**Leaves of Life
Words, Words, Words**

Also by Ian Coulls and published by Ginninderra Press
The Complete and Utter Truth About the World and Everything In It
Where the Hell Is Heaven?
Bookends
Danse Macabre (Pocket Poets)
Words (Picaro Poets)
On the Road To Somewhere Else (Picaro Poets)

Ian Coulls

Leaves of Life
Words, Words, Words

My thanks to Stephen Matthews and Brenda Eldridge of
Ginninderra Press, Rob Walker, Jules Leigh Koch, Anthony Priwer,
Chris Finnen, Darrell Coggins, Ray Clift, Christina Barrie,
Shirley Jansen, Lorna Lower and Amy Yang for their support
and encouragement.

A special word of thanks to Amy Yang for allowing her artwork on
the cover of six of my seven books.

Leaves of Life: Words, Words, Words
ISBN 978 1 76041 923 3
Copyright © text Ian Coulls 2020
Cover art: Amy Yang

First published 2020 by
GINNINDERRA PRESS
PO Box 3461 Port Adelaide 5015 Australia
www.ginninderrapress.com.au

Contents

Prelude
Poetry is Dead	11
A Night Out With Mummy	12
The Day I Left	14
The Mirror	15
The Quest	16
Hey Father	18

Fact or Fiction?
The Mark of Cain	21
The Rape of Mary	22
La Belle Saison	23
The Arrival of Godot	24
Renaissance	25

Conflict
Tightrope	29
Battlefield	31
War Zone	32
The Invisible Wound	34

Maria
Maria I	39
Maria II	40
Maria III	42
Maria IV	43
Maria V	44
Maria VI	45
Maria VII	46
Maria VIII	47
Maria IX	48
Maria X	50
Maria XI	51

Country Life

The Lone Ranger	55
When They Come to Take Me	56
The Hawk	57
The Hermit	58
Another Busy Night	59
Desert Sand	60
Hilltop Poplars	61
Birdsong	62
Valediction	63

Urban Life

Junk Mail	67
Sidewalk Serenade	68
The City	69
The City II	70
Exit	71
Talkback Radio	72
The Hidden Truth	73
The Poetry of a Visit to One's Insurance Agent	74

Judgement

Experts	77
This is Not a Poem	79
How I Coped With Yesterday	81
Not the Annual Letter	83
Download the Update	85
Measurement	86
Regal	88
Villon	89
Justice	90
To sponse or not to sponse	91

Paradise Lost

The Language of Music	95
The Wound	97
As I Lie in Bed	98
Sam	99
Silence	100
To the Child We Never Had	101
Snapshot	102
Danse Macabre	103
You're Gone	104
The Garden of Dystopia	105
Cold, Cold Moon	106
The Power of Two	107

This Final Flourish

My New Friend	111
Fly to Me	112
A Walk Through History	113
The Room	114
It's Not Geography	115
Pablo Neruda and I	117

Endgame

Time Goes By	121
Sharing	122
Jigsaw	123
Ridgididge	124
Peripheral	125
A Balanced Equation	126
Euthanasia	127
No Bell Will Ring	128
Dust to Dust	129
This One Same Day	130

Prelude

Poetry is Dead

Poetry is dead,
the song is sung,
the knights on milk-white steeds
departed with the setting sun,
the books not burnt
but bathed in dust, unloved,
lie fallow on deserted shelves.

The Common Man is come.
Still there's battle and the quest for power
but with the dagger, not the sword.
Now there is no code, no honour,
no bible of the heart.
Now there is no rainbow,
no magic in the sky,
no moon, no stars, no sunrise,
no song, no dance, no golden sunset.

Accountants now can measure joy,
pharmacists can weigh our laughter,
preachers preach forever after
but night is filled with gunshot violence,
tortured tyres pierce the silence,
no escape from sirens, screeches,
no more walks on moonlit beaches,
reaching out in heart and head
in search of words that might be said
to share another's inner world
now poetry is dead.

A Night Out With Mummy

Still, this statue in my mind,
not even that,
a photo of a statue,
the memory of my mother.

Only sometimes
in the dark of night,
in the deep dark still of night,
I hear his raised voice,
I smell the beer.

'Don, don't hit me.'

I shut my eyes
and turn away
but the noise
of what I hear
and what I fear
drags me back into the room.
He has her by the wrists
and pushes her against the wall.

'Mummy!'

He turns to see,
she struggles free
and comes to me,
sweeps me up,
still in pyjamas,
still in my blanket.
He comes at us
but I'm between.

We burst out
into the winter night.
The door slams
and mutes abuse
hurled in pursuit…

and this remains
the only living memory
of my mother.

The Day I Left

The nicer folk
would be appalled
that in the street
two men could come to blows.

The seed was sown
so long ago.
The woman that we fought about
had died nine years before.

I don't recall the reason
he slapped me in the face.
With burning ear I struck back,
a punch, not a slap.

He reeled and held his jaw.
Stunned, he raged,

'You hit your father.'

From somewhere deep inside
my answer tumbled out.

'You hit my mother.'

No further blow was struck.
No further word was said.
He turned and walked inside.
I turned and walked away.

The Mirror

Putting away
what was his,
he turned
and lurched
towards the basin,
washed his hands.

Leaning forward
he paused in horror.
Behind the mirror
a ravaged face.
For all these years
he'd thought it his…

and now he saw his father.

The Quest

Some folk like the limelight
some want to live in peace.
Some go off in search of truth,
to seek the Golden Fleece.
Some seek love in heaven
and happiness on Earth.
Some grasp for love so desperately
they strangle it at birth.

We're all such poor dumb bastards
with our doggy-doing ways,
pissing on the fence posts
and wasting our best days,
duelling on the highwire
to show that we're the best,
trying to show the heroine
we're better than the rest.

Maybe we'll get married
forever and a night,
just another reason
to start another fight.
You don't see it my way,
can't seem to think it through,
so I'll just strike out blindly
to get it through to you.

Blessed are the beautiful
it smooths the road ahead.
Blessed are the beautiful,
it puts people in their bed.
I know that it's not easy
knowing who's for real
but it's not hard to wear a smile
when you know you've got appeal.

So if you'll be my princess,
the sunrise in my east,
you, the gentle beauty,
I, the fearsome beast,
on the road to somewhere else
'cause that's the way it goes,
trying to find a place that's ours,
a place less thorn than rose,

we'll ride into the setting sun
astride my trusty steed
and, all the way, defend our cause,
the peaceful life we need,
and every day will echo
with love and joy and laughter,
and just like in the fairy tales
we'll love forever after.

Hey Father

Hey Father,
it's 6 a.m.
and I'm in Paris.
The rain descends
silently to the ground
like a lover's slip.

I can't sleep
but I don't mind.
I've walked the streets of Paris,
paid grudging respect
to its famous avenues,
sat in sidewalk bistros,
watching Gallic pride
duelling on the boulevard.

The rain becomes insistent
and the gutters
gurgle their indigestion
to the reluctant dawn.

So many moments
I'd want to share
if you were alive.

Fact or Fiction?

The Mark of Cain

To chip a rock
to make an edge,
to find a branch
to mount the point,
to glue and bind
the point and shaft
to kill a beast
to eat as food.

But then to turn
to aim the spear
to kill another,
to kill the brother
born of his mother
to take her as his lover.

Paradise sinks further
into the swamp of time.

The Rape of Mary

I hear you came to Mary
in the middle of the night.
You didn't ask,
you didn't stay
and then she bore your child.

So Joseph wasn't happy
but what could humans do?
You had your way with this young girl
who'd not yet reached full bloom.

And then you came
with rules and laws
by which we should abide…
but if future gods are women,
you'll need somewhere to hide.

La Belle Saison

August fifteen
Day of the Assumption
Mary's rise to higher ground
to see to those below.

August fifteen
the day Jacques Prévert saw you
young and hungry pavement girl
hoping for a handout.

August fifteen
Place de la Concorde
the square of liberation
symbol of the future.

Did someone come
and give you bread
take you home
give you warmth
tell you it would be all right?

Did someone come
and give you love?

Did Mary come
and lift your load?

The Arrival of Godot

On the plain
a man sits
waiting for the One Who Knows
the Truth That Blinds
the Cosmic Answer.

Above him
the skies open
and an Unknown God
laughs a Pigeon Turd.

Renaissance

The Dark Age is fading fast,
the light is flooding in.
Now Purgatory's obsolete,
they're redesigning sin.
The gargoyles now just represent
our fears in times gone past.
The curtain has been pulled back.
The fear is fading fast.

Farewell the Inquisition,
no more stakes through the heart.
It's so hard to put together,
so easy to pull apart.
Forget about the fairies
and Merlin's magic wand.
Our innocence will see us through
to whatever lies beyond.

So sweep away the cobwebs,
the ignorance and fear.
Roll on, the Renaissance,
the Age of Light is here.

Conflict

Tightrope

Now life is like a tightrope.
We walk the best we can.
Walk it like a hero,
walk it like a man.

Though someone said that things have changed
and men are not the ones.
Their hands are in their pockets
but they're not holding guns.

The gallery is filled with clowns,
they watch the heroes play,
but most of all they like the falls
though they tell themselves, 'One day…'

And sometimes when the rope's not firm,
we look round for a friend.
We look down at the faces
and we look back up again.

When we lose we're Quasimodo,
when we win we're Errol Flynn
and even when we're Errol,
we sometimes don't get in.

I saw you in the tent top,
I saw you climb the slope.
I saw you take your chances,
I saw them cut the rope.

I heard the anger of the crowd,
I heard the cry for blood.
The clowns reached for their moment
and filled their hands with mud.

But I still well remember
the time when I was down
and you were at my shoulder
when I looked around.

So I'm sitting at the station,
been here since yesterday.
I heard the people shouting
and thought you'd pass this way.

Sometimes a man must stand
for what he thinks is true.
I know what I stand for,
I know I stand for you.

Battlefield

Six months ago
I threw myself
into this trench
and cringed.

Six full months
I've hidden,
face in hands.
Sometimes I've peered
above the rim.
Still no cataclysm.

Yesterday, somewhat cramped,
I looked around and found
no one in my trench.

Today, mole-like,
I emerged,
cast my myopic vision
over the battlefield.

No craters,
no bodies,
no carrion.

Yet more assured,
I've come to like
my people-shelter.
Maybe I'll defend it
against the marauding mice.

I hereby claim this trench
in the name of the gentle people.

War Zone

If I get there
I'll be twelve tomorrow.

The street below
a sea of rubble,
bodies, weapons
bathed in gore.

From somewhere near,
the squalling of a baby,
the wailing of a mother.

Beside me,
my brother's rasping breath,
then a sickening gurgle.

The smell of shit,
stale piss and rotting flesh
heavy in the air.

I look once more
to where the playground was,
remember childhood games,
my brothers and my friends.

Now, the skeletons of field guns,
the scorched remains of army tanks.

A wounded boy
lies in the street.
I know
I can't abandon him.

Kalashnikov in hand,
I stumble down the stairs.
Halfway down,
I remember…
my brother's weapon,
his magazine of thirty rounds.

On the landing,
the tatters of a flyblown girl,
burst open like a rag doll.

The throbbing question
plagues my mind…

if we fight for God,
why are we condemned to life
in this eternal hell?

The Invisible Wound

Once a year on Turkey's shore,
teary-eyed,
they take their selfies,
don't want to know
the duty of a soldier
is the killing of the enemy.

They think the army's way is ugly,
feel that there's a nicer way
to train a man to kill.
At least it's cleaner now,
with a button, out of sight.
Your screen shows just a puff.

So when I woke,
her hand was on my cheek.
I didn't know the tear was there,
she said it was OK,
would I like to talk
and how about some coffee?

Some doctor said I shouldn't be,
so I said I wasn't angry.
'Shouldn't be angry'
made me angry
just like back then
when they forced me to salute.

He said I mustn't think that way.
I should have said,
'How come you know
what I must and mustn't?'
He'd just have said
I mustn't be like that.

Get the vet. I need the needle.
Why do people always hit me
with what I should and shouldn't?
Why am I still angry?
How come
my wife still loves me?

Maria

Maria I

One-room peasant hut
inside a couple make love
outside a child weeps.

Maria II

Maria's mother
sold herself to local folk
who didn't like outsiders.
They didn't like the lowlife
from the other side of town.

They told their wives
they disapproved
of things her mother
did with others
from the lower side of town.

Their daughters saw their mothers' dread,
the things their fathers left unsaid.
So, as she wore her mother's name,
Maria wore her mother's shame
on the other side of town.

Endlessly friendless,
she went to school
till sports day came
and they all learnt
that she was queen of the arena.

Then it was, 'Hey, we won!'
and 'Yay, Maria!'
for just one day,
but then once more
she was daughter of a whore.

And down the pub the fathers talk,
'Fourteen's too young
but give her time.
A few more years
or three more beers
and she'll be ripe.'

Maria III

Maria, you dismay me
with your fears of madness
and hopes for horseback heroes.

You come dancing
through the weeds and beer cans,
spreading love and sadness
with your knowing eyes.

You touch me
with your young dreams
of lonely beaches
and screwing your lover
in the waves of grass.

You unnerve me
with your smile.

Maria IV

Tonight
in tattered gown
he has paraded his early hours
through the deserted city.

Fifty miles of neon
have slipped across his windscreen
and now
he has come to tell her
that life is not simple.

Maria V

In the kitchen
she stands,
wearing his tattered gown,
making coffee.

In the bedroom
he lies,
wearing traces of their lust,
thinking 'bout the coffee.

Maria VI

Helpless
she wanders
from room to room,
seeking some small scrap of hope,
when every room reminds her
he was there
and now he's not.

Hopeless
she sees him
push their shared world
to the darkest corners of his mind,
leaving her
only the feeling
that life is just a death
with nothing on both sides.

Maria VII

Maria walking down the beach
Maria shrinking out of reach
walking in the morning park
gently weeping in the dark.

Fallen angel, lost in time
lost the rhythm, lost the rhyme
reflection in the wishing well
hopes of heaven, fears of hell.

Her father's touch, her childhood fears
and still more tears in later years
hanging on this cross called love
with hell below and sky above.

Between her breasts the crucifix
spelling out her politics
the tattoo on her inside thigh
waiting for some young man's eye.

Clench your teeth, clench your love
dare reach out for what's above
forbidden words, worlds forbidden
dares to share what she's kept hidden.

Virgin Mary, quite contrary
Black Madonna, Birthday Fairy
Tia Maria, altar wine
Maria Mia, rise and shine.

Maria VIII

So there again
halfway round the world
she wrestles the same old question,
who do mothers cry to?
Her little book is fat with names
of folk on whom she cannot bleed.

Then, in the early morning hours,
when emptiness swells like a haemorrhage,
there, as the flickering candles
cast towering shadows of her solitude,
she hunts in vain
through the dusty labyrinth of her life
in search of solace, warmth,
finding only names and promises.

Is this all there is of yesterday,
these musty shadows
draped with cobwebs,
this graveyard of stillborn hopes?
Where is the tattered shroud of love?

Each day
the endless smiling mask,
each night
the cruel but honest mirror
revealing only shadow.

Maria IX

If I went to Notre Dame
and there I tried to find
a helping hand, a guiding light,
some caring Master Mind,

if I went to Notre Dame
and lay there on the ground
and tried to find you peace of mind,
the peace you never found,

if I went to Notre Dame
and prayed you'd find your feet
so you could walk out in the street
weaned from the bottle's teat,

if I went to Notre Dame
to intercede for you
with fading hope that just this once
some saviour might come through,

I'd light a candle in the dark
and sit and pray for you.
I'd pray you find the god you want
and pray that he pray too.

I'd pray you find the spirit,
the strength you never knew.
You sought it in a statue
instead of inside you.

You lost it in the bottle
if it wasn't lost before.
The bottle was the battle
in which you lost the war.

And even now I think out loud
the things I'd say in prayer
and hear them melt to silence…
you'd still not know we care.

Maria X

She never said
about her trembling hands.
We never said we saw.

Maria XI

Maria was too generous.
Some offer just their hand in greeting.

So many dreams
crushed
between the ceaseless grind
of well-worn thighs.

So many men
who never cared
that brief embrace
baptised them brothers.

Now see Maria
in the ragged coat of later years,
drinking port
'midst piles of dishes,
waiting for some midnight visit
and staring at the single bullet
that finally spilt her brain.

Country Life

The Lone Ranger

From town to town with Tonto,
thriving on good deeds,
tripping out on ego
and handing out love beads.
No one knows just who he is
or where he's headed for,
if he sleeps with Tonto
or has to buy a whore.

Handing out good deals
and dealing out good hands,
sometimes playing one-night stands
in worn-out country bands.
Robin Hooding here and there
and helping people out.
No one ever asks him in
to find what he's about.

Last time I saw him
was hanging from a tree.
Someone mentioned something 'bout
his folks in Galilee.
Now Tonto's riding Silver,
got everything he needs.
He's formed a corporation
sells badges, masks and beads.

When They Come to Take Me

People tell me
my beard is greying
but I don't care.

No longer do I think
of your soft body
or the smile you borrowed from a book.

No longer do I think
of your savage lust
or the child you almost bore,

of the angry townsfolk
raking me with pitchfork eyes,
pointing me out with shotgun finger.

And when they come to take me
to their street lamp crucifixion
I won't think of you.

The Hawk

Am I like the hawk that soars
in air too rare
on the silver mantras
of sun and sky?

If I fall short of the white light,
I shall plummet
to the long grass
as if for prey
and there,
unseen by those who pass,
couched in the soft damp turf,
bathed in a thousand scents,
I'll await the void.

The Hermit

The hermit's gone
on holiday at home
and spends his time
blessing mountaineers.

Fondly suckling
delusions of grandeur
he sees the pilgrims climb.

But only I,
who have climbed
his holy mountain
so many times
to find him
kissing mirrors,

I who have
scaled his holy mind
so many times
to find it fogbound,

only I can sit back,
thumbs in belt,
and say I still don't know.

That place he goes for safety,
that altar deep inside,
is hard to find
among the clouds
that shroud his mind.

Another Busy Night

So once again he reeled home,
drunk with bitterness, drained of love,
looking for some gay new way
to pass away the time of day.

Tonight he washed his golden locks,
decided not to count his socks,
decided not to count his friends,
decided not to hump the hens,
fed the ducks the mouldy bread,
swept the floor and locked the door
and in the end, went to bed.

Desert Sand

Infinite purity
proud and timeless
forbidding, forsaken, magnificent
tidal flow defying change.

Promiscuous, masculine sand
penetrating everything.

Soft, feminine sand
swallows the intruder's feet
assimilates the foreign
swelling and ebbing like the tide
across time's spectrum
washing away all trace of man.

Hilltop Poplars

Hilltop poplars lance the sky.
Billowing grasses crown the hill,
browning and slipping down
into the valley,
down to the dry creek bed,
sandy, rock-strewn,
banked by skeletal gums.

The evensong of crickets,
a crystal chirping
gently scented
by the drought's dead sheep.

Willows stoop to drink
water which isn't there.
Beneath a desert oak
two bodies lie merged.

On the skyline
a dog lifts its leg
in salute to a poplar.

Birdsong

It's six o'clock
and not yet light.
Outside the house
their day has dawned.

Loud, impassioned,
birds fill their world with song.
They fill our hearts with music
but their songs are not for us.

Perhaps they seek a mate.

Perhaps, like cats
but mellifluous, less pungent,
they mark their boundaries.

Perhaps they sing their truth,
wasted on a world
that doesn't care.

Their life is brief
but driven by an inner plan
that spares them human care and grief.

Valediction

I know this aged land
like a long-time lover's body.

I've come to love
these rolling hills,
their pleats and creases
folding gently down
'neath a billowing sheet of grass.

Here, a paunch,
a swelling straight from Rubens,
there, a thigh
fades beyond my failing sight.

Here, a breast,
round, unclad and proud,
there, a softly grassed mound,
whose down enshrouds its hidden folds.

This has been my home.
With deep regret
I leave these lands.
They'll linger in my heart
as one remembers a former love.

Urban Life

Junk Mail

I'm waiting for this letter
from a lady that I know
but the junk mail in my post box
just grows and grows and grows.
My mailbox has a tourniquet
to try and stop the flow.

Posters from the local store
to tell me what to buy,
brochures from the car yard
inviting me to try,
pamphlets from Jehovah
'bout my future in the sky.

Satisfaction guaranteed,
our product has no peer.
Sign along the dotted line,
no payment till next year.
Never mind the small print,
just sign it here and here.

Everybody wants you
to purchase what they sell.
No charge for the guarantee,
it doesn't work too well
and if the product doesn't please,
then you can go to hell.

Sidewalk Serenade

Emerging from the subway
a fifteen-hundred-dollar suit,
a sidewalk swagger,
chooses me
and closes in,
peels back one batwing
of his jacket lining,
adorned with sachets,
plastic bags and blotting paper,
envelopes of artificial pleasure.

'Hey man,' he says,
'you want it.
I got it.'

The City

In the nitty gritty of a great big city,
the wind blowing papers round my feet,
there's a whistling in the wires
and the roaring of the tyres
as the cars go roaring down the street.

I'm arrived from out of town and I'm looking around
to see what's new to be found.
There's an all-night lady on every corner,
for a price you can follow her down.

There's a man near the gutter and he speaks with a stutter
and the whisky hits you when he speaks.
He looks a little shady but he says he knows a lady
who can keep her motor running for weeks.

There's a toothless old mess in a worn-out dress
hustling for a dollar for a meal.
There's a peacock preenin' in a black limousine 'n'
he wants to sell a mighty fine deal.

There's a place you can go, it's an all-night show
where the women lay their secrets bare
and the men come in teams and they cream their jeans
as the eyeballs roll down the stair.

The City II

In the big city it's a social whirl
but the laundromat's the same all around the world.
Plastic people, strutting round like geese
but sometimes I'm proud where I point my piece.

Stand in line if you want to be kissed.
I'm a little busy now but I'll put you on the list.
Nothing in the freezer, telly's been reclaimed,
making love on the roof, lost your earring down the drain.

There's a lady in the alley tryin' to raise her tally.
Tonight's a little slow but she's hoping things'll rally.
Tonight's a little slow for a lady in the trade
unless she gets laid by a copper on a raid.

Salvation comes in all shapes and sizes.
Don't forget your prayers and your exercises.
There's a man on the sidewalk preaching what you shoulda
but heaven's even gooder with a kilo of Buddha.

There's a man on the corner and he's selling paradise.
Give him half your money and he'll make you feel nice.
Give him half an hour and he'll teach you how to dance.
Give him half a chance and he'll dance into your pants.

The people say they love you but it isn't quite true.
Just wait until they get the knives into you.
John double-crossed Sally but she put him in his place,
put her fingers in his mouth and ripped off his face.

Exit

The chilling mist
the doorway body
lying, maybe dying.

No one dares,
no one cares
to check for life.

Death, the final secret,
life's sweet answer
to the quest for peace.

Talkback Radio

Her radio is dying.
It whistles
bristles
splutters.

It pops and crackles
but doesn't snap.
It buzzes, farts and sputters.

The voices peer out
from the long grass of static
but still she embraces
their unshaved words
their bearded offering
their shaggy wisdom.

They descend in parallel
on the long slow road to nowhere.

The Hidden Truth

Do you remember
how I sang you songs
in a foreign tongue

so your lover wouldn't know
of our hidden truth?

I find now
I sang for love
of my own voice
as you knew no French…

so your lover never knew
of our hidden lie.

The Poetry of a Visit to One's Insurance Agent

I should have read the small print
but I needed reassurance
so I got up in the night
and drove 'cross town to see their man.

I should have phoned,
he was busy with his neighbour.
I tapped her bedroom window
and called him from the garden.

I hoped they wouldn't miss the flowers
but I was feeling hungry.
Crouched in the garden
beneath her window
I ate the daisies,
relieved I had no friends to see me.

I couldn't help but ask for help
but it was hard he told me.
His neighbour laughed
and told me that he couldn't come.

So, overcome by hunger,
I finished off the daisies.

Judgement

Experts

I turn on the telly
to get the sporting news.
People looking out at me
and telling me their views.

A movie critic went to town
on someone's latest movie.
Told the world how bad it was
and thought that he was groovy.

Experts on the TV
dissect the game of cricket,
sticking penetrometers
deep into the wicket,

predicting how the balls will fly
if the batsmen snick it.
Why can't we watch in peace
and tell the press to stick it?

Experts in the schools
put wisdom in our reach.
Experts even higher up
teach teachers what to teach.

Experts in the government
tell us what to think.
Experts in the media
tell government they stink.

Experts to the left of us,
experts to the right,
experts on the racing,
experts on the fights,

experts on the weather,
experts on the war,
experts on economy,
experts on the law,

experts on environment,
experts on the whales,
experts on disarmament
and menopause in males,

experts on dining out,
experts on fine wine,
convinced that their opinion's worth
much more than yours or mine,

experts at finding fault
with the singer in the band,
experts at making love
to their favourite hand.

This is Not a Poem

These days, could be a poem
white man's rhythm
addressing social issues
histrionic gesture
mocking smugly
avoiding rhyme
just like a scandal.

So clever
to keep a straight face
while writing prose
devoid of any signs
of breath

divided
into random lines

cleverly
avoiding scansion
and the sound
of wind
and rippling water
flickering dreams
illusions
at the keyhole
of your neighbour

offering
not the faintest fragrance
of last night's passion,

so clever
that only
when you read out loud
will you know
it's not a poem.

How I Coped With Yesterday

So there I was
fronted by some rock'n'roll poet
some haircut with attitude
wants to slam me with his poetry,
me with my half-mast lungs
my flaky spine
my triple bypass
the specialist said
should be quintuple.

And what the hell does he think
he's going to prove, this lad
with his pants full of masturbation,
wanting to smack an old man about the face
with his dead-fish street-theatre poems,
some not so dapper
slammer rapper slapper
who shoots his bolt
gets up and goes home.

And then I think,
poor kid,
maybe I should help,
but I'm not so into sermons.

And then I think, hey Ian,
selfish bastard that you are,
in another time
another world
you were there,
his 'Streets of London'.

So hey,
this kid is offering you his pity
when he's just another smile
in a day that's filled with laughter.

Not the Annual Letter

No, it's not the annual letter,
the one you send to everyone,
the one in which you tell us
how the child has grown this year
and how the cat had four kittens,
three of which were drowned at birth.

It's not the letter telling how
you and your good man
go to church
on Thursday night
to practise ringing bells.

Nor will I, who write so little,
tell you of my sister's motorbike,
her boss's roving hands
or how I had to shoot my dog
when it killed the neighbour's chickens.

Nor will I tell
of that one grey morn
when, on the road,
my cat was turned to pizza.

But yesterday, I don't know why,
I thought of you
and how you've lived your life.

'Cause back there then
so few were friends,
you weren't like them.
They treated you so poorly.

They didn't see your strength…
not the strength
of those who lift things,
nor the strength
that knows no pain,
the warrior strength
of those who fight,
attracting admiration.

But there among those fine, fine folk
you faced your own Golgotha,
and wounded by their cruelty,
yet steeled by something deep inside,
you found another world,
where people take the time to care,
give more than take
and freely share.

And those who mocked in Adelaide
will never see the life you've made.

Download the Update

> She wasn't who she said she was,
> but wanted him to change.

What to do with this brief time of coming and going, of freedom and duty, of living and dying, of pain and beauty, till borne away like leaves on the breeze, food for the earth, food for the trees?

Doing the right thing from cradle to hearse, in health and wealth, for better or worse, to take your heart in your hand and sing to the stars when the gallery's interest's in clothing and cars,

to be BB King when they wanted Elvis, to be a heart that's true when they wanted your pelvis, to be Johnny O'Keefe when they wanted Madonna, to be a fashionable wanker when you valued your honour.

What happened to the magic? What happened to the fun? All your friends have bought a house and a licence for a gun. You're a knight in white armour. Here comes the embalmer. Such weary ideas. Your clock's in arrears.

These are the modern days.
These are today's new ways.

Measurement

> To seek the highest
> to remain upright and strong
> to grow stiff and snap.

Fuck you and fuck your maths
and fuck your quantum wank.
What's love in a vacuum?
Can you store it in a tank?

Show me the graph
of the feeling in your song.
The arc of your life,
is it short or is it long?

Do you have a map
of the journey of your life?
What's the algebraic sum
of a husband and a wife?

God bless the mathematics
of her nipples in your lips,
the geometry of loving,
of intertwining hips.

The age of a man
isn't measured by the clock.
The measure of the man
is not the measure of his cock.

Nor can love be measured
by the promises he's spent.
In his mind it's always Mardi Gras,
in his pocket always Lent.

Now here comes plasticity
measuring our platonicity,
our feelings' elasticity,
the sum
of authenticity,
the weight
of electricity,
the age
of eccentricity,
the height
of current fashion,
the depth
of someone's passion.

So put away your slide rule,
your hammer and your nails.
Happiness cannot be fixed
with measurement or scales.

Regal

Regal,
a heavenly premonition,
she glides toward us.
In deference,
the road kowtows
beneath her.

Like an ocean liner,
she doesn't see
our minor craft,
like bobbing gulls
before her.

On approach
she hawks
and from a great height
a diamond gob
lobs at our feet.

Villon

Où sont les neiges d'antan?

Hey François,
I'm glad they didn't get you.
Just like Rimbaud
you said your say and disappeared.

They would have strung you up.
They didn't like your kind,
the things you did,
the theft, the quarrels.

Maybe some were iffy,
but things you said
have rung down through the ages,
words like photos,
painted portraits,
your head, your heart, your times,
the folk you knew,
the world you drew,
the drunkards and the whores,
the brothels and the laws.

Your life was never boring,
the drinking
and the whoring.

'Where are the snows of yesteryear?'

Justice

And they slew him
with the anger
of those who've sold their soul,
saying,

'Who was he to differ?'

And in the morning
on the road
when he was just a bloody stain
they walked on by,
saying,

'Praise the Lord!
Justice has been done.'

To sponse or not to sponse

So much to give
but no one wants it.
As the sponsingest sponsor
I'd have loved to sponse it.

Paradise Lost

The Language of Music

She read anything with dots.
If beneath your polka-dotted dress
your breasts would bounce,
her pitch would rise and fall.

How strange
that lines and dots
could, through her eyes
and through her hands,
weave such music,
craft such magic,
these dots painted by another hand,
painted by another man,
who spoke a different tongue,
created in another land,
another age,
reaching out across the years
and touching many hearts.

How strange
so many hearts can beat in time
to a song from long ago,
to these patterns on a page.

And yet
without these dots
the song would fade and die,
her hands would come to rest
and hearts would sing no more.

How strange
when hearts reach out
and touch with words unspoken,
how people's lives embrace in tune,
entwine in time and harmonise.

and yet
without the heart
their song would fade and die,
their life would come to rest
and love would sing no more.

The Wound

Last night I saw your wound.
I too am tortured by twisted history,
by the proud flesh
that torments me at night.

Let's marry our wounds together
that we may live
as one awesome Siamese monster.

Let's share our wounds
and marry our flesh
as some small comfort
against the world.

The years may set our common scar
like some mystic crystal
to shine on those around us,
that the deeds of those we know
may be the children of our wound.

As I Lie in Bed

As I lie in bed
I can't help but think
of the firm round breasts
you thought too small,
of the soft warm body
you thought I might not want.

I think how you drew me to you,
so different from those women
who surrender like a cavalry charge.

Gossamer, ivory,
moonbeams, crystal, sunlight,
these were the shades
you lent our love.

And after,
bathed in the scent of our passion,
your lips discovered my body,
so unlike those women
whose caresses could iron overalls.

Sam

Farewell Sam.
So easy to love,
you were here and gone
so quickly,
giving us this one brief day
of fruitless plans
and leaving us
those corners of our lives,
so willingly conceded,
that still remain
untouched.

Silence

Once again,
in the silent womb of night,
a distant pulse to harmonise
with what we store inside.

Too numb to feel,
too dumb to speak,
too dry to bleed,
too drunk to drink,

staring from the balcony,
the balcony of the mind,
to hear this throbbing
silence in our ears,

this dream we have,
this song unsung,
this deed not done,
this word unspoken…

Silence.

To the Child We Never Had

I think I'll need to be around
to help you when you see
what utter bastards folk can be,
a bit like you, a bit like me.

We'd better soon get started
if I'm to lend a hand,
if you're half the turd that I was
before being half a man.
I love your mother far too much
to leave her struggling here alone
with someone we've created,
to raise the seed we've sewn.

And if in time I fade and die
and sometimes in the dark you lie
and wonder who I was,
I'll need to leave you traces
of moments and of places,
I'll need to leave you telltale clues
in case you ever wonder who's
the man who left you here.

I'll need to help your mother,
to see her through, supporting you
on your road to who knows where.
I'll need to leave you bits of me,
some tattered scraps of history,
to show I really cared.

Snapshot

Frozen in time,
staring down the barrel
of my lover's smoking gun,
I see this snapshot moment.

Numb with disbelief,
the crippling question
blazing through my brain,
I turn to see
beneath the whirlpool ceiling
the splatter on the wall behind,
the shredded tatters
of my paradise.

And in my butchered mind
this one last time
the tortured corpse of love
sinks to its knees.

Danse Macabre

You come and go
and tune my naked love
with dates and times.
But the strings slip,
the chord turns sour
and the song dies.

I could have lived without you
but you came again
with promises of tomorrow.

And now,
fragile as a new idea,
I sit awake
listening to the milkman
and cats rutting in the street.

Peering through a misty window
I watch the *danse macabre,*
the splinters of my life
lodging in no one's flesh.

Like some loose hubcap come adrift
I roll the streets of life,
clanking madly through the early hours,
dancing mad circles on people's doorsteps
and rattling off
the catechism of dereliction.

You're Gone

The cat's not coping
the garden's moping
you're gone.

The flame tree's pining
the pine tree's flaming
you're gone.

December remembers
September's embers
you're gone.

The Garden of Dystopia

Help me hold my world down.
Sanity floats away
and madness stalks the garden.

I can't control the spinach…

The turnips answer back…

I see some crazy jigsaw
where I drop IOUs
into a wishing well…

where I play fantasias
on a harp that's strung with cobwebs…

where I surround myself
with a thousand mirrors
that remain cold and indifferent
to my chronic myopia.

Come sit beside me
so I can return in peace
to the nurture of my navel.

Cold, Cold Moon

Cold, cold moon, light my night.
A distant ghost, your phantom light,
indifferent to all tales of woe,
a reflection of the cold below,
shines through the clouds to help our sight,
casts shadows on both wrong and right,
guides our path for what it's worth
till we are stardust here on Earth.

The Power of Two

I struggle in these sunset hours
I would have spent with you.
The richness of life's treasure
is double shared by two
and better if we're lovers
the way it used to be
and better if you want to share
the rest of life with me.

And sometimes on the long, long haul
to the other side of night
we'd shelter from the world
till morning's early light.
Stereo is better,
life's richer to the power of two.
If ever there were paradise
I thought it there with you.

This Final Flourish

My New Friend

You brushed the snowflakes,
the burden from my shoulders.
Hello, my new friend.

With such ease you breached
ramparts built to keep me safe.
I have no defence.

Fly to Me

Fly to me, little bird
time is short
the spring is gone
the grass is dry.

The flowers you left have wilted
stay this long last blazing summer
and share the jacaranda evenings.

Come to me
in the crushing silence
of the early hours
and fill the void
with wordless songs
of sweet release,
where heart and mind
flesh and feeling
space and time
all merge with night.

With the coming of the winter
you must fly
and I must sleep.

Come share the night
this one last time
until the hourglass drains.

A Walk Through History

Strolling
through my history,

scrolling
the tales a garden tells,

she sees the relics,
the melaleuca amputation,
the cathedral of our pine.

She hears our birdsong,
mouths the words
that name the birds
in a tongue that stumbles
but persists.

She wanders
through the growth and death,
pictures time gone by,
wonders who and when and why.

She sees her place in history,
and knows that she's at home.

The Room

Here, in this tiny room,
in this crypt in time and space,
here in this nest of ants,
this homeless human race,

homeless, hopeless, lost in time,
looking for the golden rhyme,
rhymeless, timeless, lost in hope,
looking for the golden dope,

dopeless, hopeless, lost in dreams,
something new, something old,
looking for a world that seems
better, brighter, bound in gold,

golder, bolder, bound in hope,
looking for the dream that seems
long and strong to climb the slope,
long and strong to climb the slope…

here, in this tiny room,
I love you.

It's Not Geography

Some seek love in heaven,
some seek love in mist,
some think love is doing things
like getting laid or kissed.

Men seek love between the thighs
and speak of length or size
while I sit on the balcony
and share my love's moonrise.

Sunrise, sunset, moonrise, moonglow,
don't ask me what I know
I know I knew before we two
were lovers, long ago.

And now my love swells like the tide
with daily ebb and flow
I share my life with you, my love,
most everywhere we go,

like in my head and in your heart
and on the breeze outside
and in the trees and on the seas
and in our bed and on our knees,

the different moods and feelings
when we're lying side by side
and watching hotel ceilings
when our love's not at high tide.

And in the safety of my hand
the murmur of your breast,
the measured heartbeat of your world
with me your treasured guest.

And when your passion rises
with the coming of the tide
you hold me close and melt away
and heaven opens wide.

You take me in and we are one
in body, soul and mind.
We're here and there and everywhere
but nowhere that they'll find.
And I'm the centre of your world
and you're my universe.
And I'm the centre of your world
and you're my universe.

Pablo Neruda and I

'I want you to know one thing,'
Neruda wrote
and told a woman
his love was true
so long as she loved him.

I've never loved that way.
The loves I've known
have never died,
just the man I was
or the woman loved.

With the passage of time
we all change
and I can't regret
the passing of the man I was.

But each new love
has seen me grow,
grow to know
the man I am.

Each new love
has led to this,
this late, late bloom.

This last flourish
has led me now to you
and in my midnight hour
one burst of glory
like the final flare
from a sinking ship.

Endgame

Time Goes By

So when at last
we turn to clay,
when night wins out
against the day,
when flesh and bone
have turned to dust
and sword and might
have turned to rust,

when love and hatred
on the breeze
are borne away
like waves on seas,
when we are gone
like mist in sky,
what will it mean
that time goes by?

Sharing

There were those
who shared our life
but never knew.

There were those who knew
but never cared to share.

And what we shared
and how we cared
were not the same,

and what we thought
and what we felt
were flood and flame,

were there and gone
on the tides of life
and winds of time.

Jigsaw

Seek me if you seek my love.
Gather debris gently.
Then make your mind a scalpel
and rearrange me mentally.

See the surgeon softly saw
and set with mucilage,
stand back, admire his handiwork,
his jigsaw fret collage.

And if the face you finally see
does not resemble mine
then strip away the pieces
and try another time.

And if the man you thought you knew
is shattered from your life
like a teacup 'neath a hacksaw,
a zeppelin on a knife,

then write for me no histories,
don't fret away or pine.
Just mark a number on my grave
and drink a glass of wine.

Ridgididge

This is it,
filled to the brink,
last night's coffee
on the sink,
this morning's muesli
in the fridge,
the Sum of Life,
ridgididge.

Your optimism's way too bold.
Don't try and tell me you weren't told.
One day you'll wake and find me cold.
That's the problem getting old.

Peripheral

Be patient, flesh,
you'll soon be gone,
a distant thought
to those who knew,
not even that
to those who didn't.

No more these hands that couldn't.
No more this will that wouldn't.

My outside world
is bathed in mist.

My inside world asks
who was that?
Why did I come?
How could that be?
What was it called?
Where's the whatsit?
What the fuck?
Who put the kettle in the fridge?

And so I ask
will memory of me
be just like passing wind,
a brief distraction,
peripheral
to everything?

A Balanced Equation

First line: the doctor said,
'We need a triple bypass.'
My question in reply,
'You mean we're both not well?'

Next line: I thought,
well, just in case,
catch up with folk
and tell them
see you later.

Third line: I asked,
they didn't visit much before,
so why would they come later?

Fourth line: the question,
why farewell folk
who never came to say hello?

Last line: I laughed,
worse comes to worst
there won't be a later.

The algebra of life and death,
left and right hand side,
equation balanced.

Euthanasia

The future is over.
Commit me to the pit of time.
The mythology in which you wrap yourself
protects you from reality.

Let me die, you hypocrite,
peeling off your rosary,
your sanctimonious smile,
your platitudes a blanket
that smothers me
and hides my pain.

You offer consolation.
I feel desolation.
You offer me your dream.
Well, come and share my nightmare.
You offer me your god.
Well, come and share my hell.

Your bedside smile,
your pulpit tone,
your understanding of eternity
assure me of my future,
my place in endless time.

But do I have a funeral plan?
Do I need insurance?
Have I done the paperwork?

No Bell Will Ring

We are so quickly history
and sometimes merely dust.
Our armour quickly tarnished,
our sword is turned to rust.

No bell will ring
when my time's come.
No band will march
to muffled drum.

No choir will sing,
no pipe will skirl,
no bugle call,
no flags unfurl.

No mourning crowds
will bow their head
and see me off
when I am dead.

No band will play that final day
when in the ground
they lay me down,
alone to turn to clay.

Dust to Dust

> Through spring and summer, autumn rain,
> through winter pain, through every vein
> till facing death with dying breath
> my heart still calls your name.

Dust to dust,
ash to ash,
when on the wind
our lives are cast
to mingle and entwine in death,
to blend as one and none.

When I am gone
I'll wait for you
till you join me there in death,
and as in life, we one flesh were,
in death we'll join as dust
till those who love us set us free,
release us on the tide of time,
scattered but still one.

Thus will our ashes, our remains,
the dust of what we've been,
on wind and water
merge in death,
make love into eternity.

This One Same Day

This one same day has come so far
around the world so many times
to sweep away the falling leaves,
the unheard songs, the fading rhymes.

Still so fresh and yet so old,
it brings us warmth but leaves us cold,
until one day it comes to pass,
but cannot reach us 'neath the grass.

www.ingramcontent.com/pod-product-compliance
Lightning Source LLC
Chambersburg PA
CBHW070917080526
44589CB00013B/1333